SUFFERING

'Why, silent God, why?'

Chris Wright
Sue Haines

LION EDUCATIONAL
Oxford · Batavia · Sydney

Copyright © 1991 Chris Wright and Sue Haines

Published by
Lion Publishing plc
Sandy Lane West, Oxford, England
ISBN 0 7459 2056 X
Albatross Books Pty Ltd
PO Box 320, Sutherland, NSW 2232, Australia
ISBN 0 7324 0497 5

First edition 1991

Design
Simon Jenkins

Quotations
We are grateful to those who have agreed to speak for their
faith; they cannot of course represent all views held by
adherents to the faith concerned.

We are also grateful to publishers and copyright holders for
permission to reproduce copyright material. The sources are as
follows:
Page 4: C. S. Lewis, *The Problem of Pain*, Collins
Page 5 (and pages 11, 31): Margaret Spufford, *Celebration*,
HarperCollins Publishers
Page 6: Margaret Drabble, *Millstone*, Penguin Books
Page 8 (and pages 21, 23, 27, 30, 32): David Watson, *Fear No
Evil*, Hodder and Stoughton Limited
Page 10: Evelyn Underhill, *Letters*, Longmans Green
Page 11: Cicely Saunders, *Beyond All Pain*, SPCK (and
page 16); Ladislaus Boros, *Pain and Providence*, Search Press
Page 12 (and pages 13, 24): Rabbi Harold Kushner, *When bad
things happen to good people*, Pan Books
Page 15 (and pages 26, 31): Frances Young, *Face to Face*,
T &T Clark Ltd
Page 17: Jim Cotter, *Through Desert Places*, Cairns
Publications
Page 18: Elie Wiesel, *A Jew Today*, Vintage Books
Page 21: Jan Thompson, *Reflections*, Hodder and Stoughton
Publishers (and page 22); Joni Eareckson, *Joni*, Marshall
Pickering (and pages 24, 28, 30)
Page 22: Frances Parsons, *Pools of Fresh Water*, SPCK/
Triangle
Page 24: Richard Holloway, *The Sidelong Glance*, Darton,
Longman and Todd
Page 25: Helen Waddell, *Peter Abelard*, Constable
Page 26: A. M. Hunter, *Introducing the New Testament*, SCM
Press; George Carey in *The Lion Handbook to Christian Belief*,
Lion Publishing
Page 29: Mother Teresa in *The Love of Christ*, Collins; Debra
Jarvis, *HIV Positive*, Lion Publishing

Bible quotations are from the following versions: Good News
Bible, page 15; Jerusalem Bible, pages 18, 19 (Psalms); New
English Bible, pages 18–19; Revised Standard Version, pages
8, 17, 31. All are used by kind permission of the copyright
holders.

A catalogue record for this book is available
from the British Library

Printed in Malta

CONTENTS

INTRODUCTION

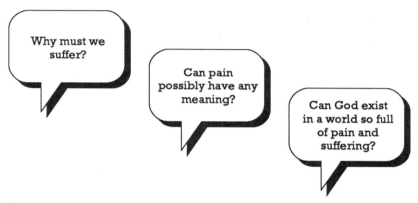

These questions will not go away. They have found their echoes in the hearts of millions of people down the centuries. Every age is marred by hate and suffering. And so people continue to ask questions which can neither be satisfactorily answered nor dismissed.

Why suffering?

Before you begin reading, take a few moments to think...and to share...situations in which people have endured terrible suffering. It may be something personal to you, your family or friends, or it could be happening in a different part of the world.

What has caused the suffering?

WHY DO GOOD PEOPLE SUFFER?

WHERE IS HE?

I'd like to see God.
I'd like to tell him a few things.
I'd like to say:
'God, why do you create people
and make them suffer and fight in vain,
and live brief unhappy lives like pigs,
and make them die disgustingly,
and rot?

God, why do
the beautiful girls you create
become whores, grow old and toothless,
die and have their corpses rot
so that they are a stench
to human nostrils?

God, why do you permit
thousands and millions of your creatures,
made in your image and likeness,
to live like crowded dogs
in slums and tenements,
while an exploiting few
profit from the sweat of their toil,
produce nothing,
and live in kingly mansions?

God, why do you permit people
to starve, hunger, die from syphilis,
cancer, consumption?
God, why do you not raise
one little finger to save mankind
from all the...suffering
on this human planet?'

That's what I'd say to God
if I could find him hiding behind a tree.
But God's a wise guy.
He keeps in hiding!

*I*n this book we explore how different people have 'come at' their own questions in order to be able to live with their suffering. In this unit we simply attempt to state the problem.

In her book *Celebration*, Margaret Spufford raises the problem in relation to the suffering of her daughter from cystinosis, a very rare, genetically-caused, metabolic disease. It is life-threatening. The following extract is taken from the part of the book where she is recounting the time spent in the Hospital for Sick Children:

> **Now the existence of Belsen and its like, that is, of humanly-created evil, I could, as a historian, cope with intellectually.** Genetic evil, creation malfunctioning from birth or from conception (as it was in my daughter's case), was more than I could account for or understand. These children suffered – and small children suffer very acutely, and worse, because no explanation is possible to them – because they were *made wrong*.
>
> The evidence of divine activity in, and through, creation and the minute ways we share in it has always been particularly important to me. Now here I was, living week after week surrounded by the evidence of failed creation, the rejections of our heavenly Father, the pots on which the potter's hand did indeed seem to have slipped.
>
> I think the bottom came for me one day when I tried to comfort a tiny anguished child (words are useless, only touch will do), and as I reached out to stroke his head a nurse said hastily, 'Don't touch him, his skull might fracture.' That same day a 'pious' friend called, and said enviously, 'Your faith must be such a comfort to you.' It was not. Belief in an omnipotent and all-loving Creator who is capable of producing results like those I was observing, produced for me at least as many problems as it solved.
>
> So there was I, a Christian, committed to the doctrine of a loving, omnipotent Father, a Creator. And there was I, living in surroundings which persistently denied this omnicompetence, amongst the 'failures' of His creation.

THINKING IT THROUGH

➡ Some people say that there cannot be a God if there is so much suffering. What do you think?

➡ What reasons could a good God have for allowing a world to exist with both good and bad in it?

➡ Look again at the poem *Where is He?* How does this make you feel? If you were able, what questions would you like to ask God?

OURS NOT TO QUESTION WHY:
A Buddhist perspective on suffering

> I could not help but ask; I had no hope of an answer, having always known that there is no answer, but it seemed to me that this woman would at least understand the terms of my question.
>
> Margaret Drabble, *Millstone*

Rosamund, the questioner in the quotation, is sitting helplessly in a hospital canteen while her innocent baby suffers in a nearby ward. In Rosamund we are confronted with the agonies of an anxious mother; as she waits for her little baby, she recognizes the uselessness of explanations but cried out for comfort, for understanding.

There is a great difference between talking about the 'issue of suffering' as a detached observer, when we are comfortably healthy, and the agonized cries of the sufferer. In the midst of suffering we cannot afford the luxury of debating the pros and cons of the 'logical problem of suffering'. The sufferer needs a more practical way of dealing with his or her own suffering, of coming to terms with it.

The Buddha recognized this need. His response to suffering was a practical way of coping with the facts, rather than a theoretical attempt to explain or justify the presence of so much suffering in the world. An incident from his life, *The Story of the Mustard Seed*, (opposite) illustrates this shift in emphasis.

RISING ABOVE SUFFERING

For the Buddha, theoretical questions on suffering serve no useful purpose. It is like the wounded man who refuses to have the arrow removed from his side until he knows who fired it, from what distance, with what kind of bow, etc. That man would die without knowing any of the answers. This approach to suffering reflects the Buddha's own life-experiences, his sudden confrontation with the existence of suffering in the form of a sick person, an old person and a corpse. His response was not to ask theoretical questions but to look for a way to rise above suffering.

In this teaching on suffering the Buddha saw himself as a doctor who diagnoses the illness and then offers a cure. His teaching is contained in the FOUR NOBLE TRUTHS:

1. Suffering (Dukkha) touches everything in life. Instead of running smoothly, life is filled with disappointments, illness, death, conflict. There is a general feeling of unsatisfactoriness and restlessness. For example, to want something badly is suffering.

2. **Unsatisfactoriness (suffering) is caused by desire (i.e. craving after things).** If we didn't become attached to things (our health, our wealth, other people) we wouldn't suffer when they are taken away. It is the feeling that we have a right to things that makes us suffer when they are no longer ours. The Buddha pointed to a 'stop craving and relax' mentality.

3. **Suffering will end when we stop craving after things.**

4. **The cure.** To stop craving, and thus suffering, we must follow the Eightfold Path which aims at disciplining our life in a positive way.

THE STORY OF THE MUSTARD SEED

There was a woman, named Gotami, whose child had just died. She was so upset by this that she lost her reason completely. She went everywhere trying to bring her child back to life. Her friends felt sorry for her and said, 'Gotami, you should go and see the Buddha. Perhaps he can help you.' Thus she went before the Buddha still holding her child in her arms. 'Please bring him back to life for me,' she cried. Very gently the Buddha answered her: 'I can help you, Gotami, but first you must bring me something. I need one small mustard seed. However, it must come from a house where no one has ever died.'

Gotami quickly went in search of a mustard seed. Wherever she went, though, the same thing happened. Everyone wanted to help her, but in every family she visited someone had died. One person told her, 'Three years ago I lost my daughter.' Another said, 'My brother died here yesterday.' It was always the same.

At the end of the day she returned to the Buddha. 'What have you found, Gotami?' he asked. 'Where is your mustard seed? And where is your son? You are not carrying him any longer.' She answered, 'O Buddha, today I have discovered that I am not the only one who has lost a loved one. Everywhere people have died. I see how foolish I was to think I could have my son back. I have accepted his death, and this afternoon I buried him. Now I have returned to you to hear your teachings. I am ready to listen.'

➡ Looking back at what Rosamund said: how might *understanding* someone's suffering differ from providing an explanation?

➡ According to the Buddha, if we did not become attached to things we would not suffer when they are taken away. It is the feeling that we have a right to things that makes us suffer when they are no longer ours. Try examining the truth of this idea by listing examples of suffering that fit this explanation.

THE DARK SIDE OF THE PICTURE

As you look around the world you can collect evidence of so much that is wrong: wars, injustice, oppression… the list is endless. Certainly at times the world can appear to be a very dark place. How could a loving God have created such a world?

The Bible does not formulate a theory to explain where all this darkness comes from. Instead, it tells a story known as 'the Fall'. The origin or reason for suffering is traced back to the beginning. The first chapters of the Bible present a story of how a perfect world created by God was spoiled.

The story of God creating a world that is good is told in the first two chapters of Genesis:

'In the beginning God created…and God saw everything that he had made, and behold, it was very good.'

However, chapter three describes the darker side of the picture: people rebel against God's creative authority and are forced to bear the consequences.

A number of important things emerge from these stories:

➡ God designed and made a world that was perfect.
➡ God created men and women with free will – the ability to choose. He did not want them to be senseless robots.
➡ Mankind chose to rebel – they wanted their own way, not God's.
➡ The price was conflict, suffering and death – a spoiling of the relationship between God and humankind which had fatal consequences for the whole of creation.

David Watson wrote *Fear No Evil* during the last year of his life. As he lay dying of cancer he attempted to write of his beliefs in an attempt to explain why he had to suffer:

❝ God can do anything, and theoretically could have programmed us as robots, impervious to pain and unable to inflict it on others. Had he done so, life might have been simpler, but there would also have been no feeling, no freedom, no relationships, no love – nothing of those human qualities which make life worth living. Instead, God has made us with a genuine freedom of choice to go his way or ours; and because we have all naturally gone our way instead of his, we live in a fallen

world which is still often staggeringly beautiful but which is sadly marred by sin, suffering and death. God has therefore entered our world in Christ and suffers with us. **99**

This quotation and the one in the margin speak of what it is like living in a spoiled world. However, the consequence of the Fall is more far-reaching than individual suffering. This spoiling has three strands:

➡ **Broken relationships between humanity and God.** Instead of living in harmony with God, men and women are only too aware of

---

WHY DOESN'T GOD STOP WAR?

Why doesn't God stop war? How?
What options are open to Him?
He's tried reasoning with mankind! He even said once, 'Come, let us reason together!'
He has tried law and order, introducing laws such as 'Thou shalt not kill', and 'Love your enemies'.
Has mankind taken any notice?

So, what other options are open to God?
Two? Exterminate all persons responsible for war, or turn mankind into a race of robots?

God could only stop war this way by stopping people, and he'd have to exterminate us all.

Or, God could turn us all into computerised beings, capable only of doing what is good and right. He could rob each of us of our freedom to choose to do wrong. After all people *do* choose to make war! God's big problem, however, is that He loves us! Despite what mankind is, despite all that we have done, God loves us too much to take up either of these two options.

So, He continues to try gentle persuasion.
He sent Jesus to show mankind that it is possible to love one's enemies! Jesus forgave and prayed for the men who were putting Him to death!

Our problem is that we think we can solve our problems without God's help.

But history, especially recent history, tells us just how well we are doing – YUK!

Jane Grayshon – a young woman with a family – has had twenty operations in the last fourteen years. She asks 'Is it wise to trust in a loving God?'

I sometimes feel that maybe God has asked me to be prepared to go through the suffering to show that when we do have very bad times it doesn't mean that God has deserted us, but that it's part of the fact that we're on earth and not in heaven.

Encounter, ITV, 12.1.91

their alienation from him – often aware of an attraction towards God and yet feeling a chasm of separation. This relationship could be restored only when God himself stepped into human history in the person of his Son, Jesus Christ (see units 8 and 9). So people often feel as if God is hidden from them, and that they are offered only hints and glimpses of his presence. No longer do they walk together through the Garden (Genesis 3:8).

➡ **Broken relationships between people.** Instead of living as one family, people have become rivals and enemies.

➡ **A spoiled relationship with the good earth.** The harmony which God planned has been shattered. Instead of being stewards of the earth we abuse it, pollute it and threaten to destroy it!

On one level it is correct to say that these are the consequences of humanity rebelling against God, illustrating their ability to choose freely. However, to leave the explanation at this level would be to miss out part of the total picture. According to the biblical story, it was Satan, a rebellious angel from God, who prompted human rebellion.

➡ One writer questions the free-will argument in the following way:

> We can't, I think, attribute all the evil and pain of creation to man's rebellious will. Its far-reaching results, the suffering of innocent nature, the imperfection and corruption that penetrate all life, seem to forbid that. The horrors of inherited insanity, mental agonies, the whole economy of disease, especially animal disease, seem to point beyond man to some fundamental disharmony between creation and God. I sympathise a good deal with the listener who replied to every argument on the love of God by the simple question, 'What about cancer in fish?'

Evelyn Underhill, *Letters*

How well do you think the argument from free will explains all forms of suffering?

➡ In view of mankind's free will, how are we to picture God? Can he remain omnipotent?

THE MYSTERY OF SUFFERING

Some people argue that it is impossible to find any meaning to suffering... it is a mystery. This chapter sets out to explore the mysteriousness of suffering. Some of the extracts we have chosen presume a belief in God, others do not.

The quest by some for meaning in the midst of suffering becomes a heartfelt cry:

> I do not beg You to reveal to me the secret of Your ways – I could not bear it. But show me one thing; show it to me more clearly and more deeply: show me what this, which is happening at this very moment, means to me, what it demands of me, what You, Lord of the world, are telling me by way of it. Ah, it is not why I suffer, that I wish to know, but only whether I suffer for Your sake.

Levi Yitzchak of Berditchev, quoted in Cicely Saunders, *Beyond All Pain*

Peter Lippert wrote:

> There are some who know everything, who penetrate even your great thoughts and decrees and give a nice, tidy explanation of them all. They explain and prove to me that it has to be just so and is best as it is. But I cannot endure these people who explain everything, who justify and find excuses for everything you do. I prefer to admit that I don't understand. That I cannot grasp why you created pain, why so much pain, such raging, crazy and meaningless pain. I bow down before your glory indeed; but I do not now venture to raise my eyes to you. There is too much grief and weeping in them. So I cannot look on you.

Quoted in Ladislaus Boros, *Pain and Providence*

In the following extract, Margaret Spufford attempts to tease out why suffering is a mystery.

> I was surrounded on the metabolic wards by the failures of creation, the drop-outs of natural selection. But the language of science, and of natural selection, and the language of theological belief in a loving, omnipotent Creator, have to be reconciled. Can they be? Here was the crux of my

A Jew responded to the atrocities of Auschwitz in these words:

> The executioner killed for nothing, the victim died for nothing. No God ordered the one to prepare the stake, nor the other to mount it. At Auschwitz the sacrifices were without point. If the suffering of one human being has any meaning, that of six million has none.

problem. These drop-outs were human babies, with all the needs of normal babies. I am never going to be able to forget the sound of those screams.

I cannot reconcile the images of tiny, deformed children with old men's eyes, in great pain (children who shrank from human contact because so often it represented more pain, the stab of a therapeutic needle which they could not recognize as therapeutic) with what I am bound to believe of a loving, omnipotent Father. I will not assent to all this pain as anything but a manifest evil. One of the commonest Christian heresies is surely to glorify suffering as somehow 'good'.

In three successive generations – my mother's, my own and my daughter's – I have known physical evil. Two of those three times it was caused by fundamental metabolic defects, and of those two times one was caused by an error in the genetic coding itself. I have searched for a theological answer. I do not believe there is one. Would, or can, any theologian produce any answer other than that we are here in the presence of a mystery, insoluble in human terms?

Why is suffering stamped indelibly all through creation like this, endemic everywhere?

While it is sometimes possible to see a cause for the suffering, it often seems to happen completely at random. For example, in the case of a plane crash killing 300 people, how can we account for the 301st passenger who missed the flight because of a flat tyre?

Rabbi Harold Kushner, *When bad things happen to good people*, in a chapter entitled 'Sometimes there is no reason', paints the following picture of humanity being still in the on-going process of creation, the creative act being seen as the creating of order out of chaos (Genesis 1:1-3ff):

… suppose God didn't quite finish by closing time on the afternoon of the sixth day? Suppose that Creation, the process of replacing chaos with order, were still going on … In the biblical metaphor of the six days of Creation, we would find ourselves somewhere in the middle of Friday afternoon. Man was just created a few 'hours' ago. The world is mostly an orderly predictable place, showing ample evidence of God's thoroughness and handiwork, but pockets of chaos remain.

In Milton Steinberg's words, we live amongst 'the still unremoved scaffolding of the edifice of God's creativity'.

THINKING IT THROUGH

In this chapter we have been looking at the idea that suffering is a mystery. Along the way, some important concepts and questions have been raised which will need to be considered later as we read other extracts:

➡ Is there any purpose to suffering?
➡ Is there such a thing as innocent suffering?
➡ If so, what does the existence of innocent suffering say about the nature of God?

What do you think?

'I cannot endure these people who explain everything…I prefer to admit that I don't understand.'

Why do you think explanations sometimes repulse the sufferer?

Rabbi Kushner wrote this tender postscript two years after his 14-year-old son, Aaron, died from progeria, a disease producing rapid ageing and death in children:

I believe in God. But I do not believe the same things about Him that I did years ago… I recognize His limitations. He is limited in what He can do by laws of nature and human moral freedom. I no longer hold God responsible for illnesses, accidents and natural disasters, because I realise that I gain little and lose so much when I blame God for those things. I can worship a God who hates suffering but cannot eliminate it, more easily than I can worship a God who chooses to make children suffer and die, for whatever exalted reasons. I guess my (car) bumper sticker reads 'My God is not cruel; sorry about yours'. God does not cause our misfortunes. Some are caused by bad luck, some are caused by bad people, and some are simply an inevitable consequence of our being human and being mortal, living in a world of inflexible natural laws. The painful things that happen to us are not punishments for our misbehaviour, nor are they in any way part of some grand design on God's part. Because the tragedy is not God's will, we need not feel hurt or betrayed by God when tragedy strikes. We can turn to Him for help in overcoming it, precisely because we can tell ourselves that God is as outraged by it as we are.

When bad things happen to good people

13

THE STORY OF SUFFERING JOB

About 500 years before Christ (or so it is thought) a man was wrestling with the problem of good people suffering while evil people prospered. Out of his questions he wrote what we know today as the Book of Job. It stands at the heart of the Old Testament, as one of the profoundest attempts to confront the issue of why God allows good people to suffer: it is one response to the mystery of suffering.

The book tells the story of 'a man named Job, living in the land of Uz, who worshipped God and was faithful to him. He was a good man, careful not to do anything evil' (1:1). Right from the beginning we are given the impression that this is the story of an exemplary figure who stands for all that is good and righteous. In this 'once-upon-a-time story about a good man who suffered', there are two main scenes: the council of heaven; Job's farm on earth.

One day, the story begins, God and Satan hold council in heaven. Satan recounts how sinful humanity is. In reply, God counsels Satan to look at Job who has done no wrong and is faithful to God. Satan holds that the only reason Job is so good and holy is because everything is going well for him – he has nothing to curse God for: he is both healthy and wealthy. However, 'Suppose you take away everything he has – he will curse you to your face!' (1:11). So the Lord said to Satan, 'All right, he is in your power, but you are not to kill him' (2:6).

So Satan leaves the heavenly council to create havoc on earth. Job's servants are killed by raiders, his children by a hurricane wind. His camels are stolen and he is cursed with sores and boils which cover his whole body. However, 'In spite of everything he suffered, Job said nothing against God' (2:10).

In the three series of poetic dialogues which follow, the author shows how Job's friends and Job himself react to these disasters.

JOB'S FRIENDS...	JOB HIMSELF...
state and restate with increasing anger a traditional defence of God's goodness and power. Basically their message is: 'Don't lose faith...God is just...he punishes the wicked and rewards the righteous. God is always just and powerful.' Their arguments are in 4:7-11; 8:1-7; 11:13-20; 22:1-14, 21-30.	is offended by the implications of what his friends say. He knows that neither he nor his children were so evil as to deserve this fate. God cannot be both all-powerful and good if he lets this happen. For his line of argument look at 6:14-15; 9:1-4, 10, 15; 10:1-2, 7; 16:1-8.

After three rounds of a dialogue in which Job voices his complaint while his friends defend God's might and goodness, the book comes to a climax in which Job pronounces his innocence (chapters 29-30) and challenges God, his accuser, either to appear with evidence against him or else to admit that he has suffered wrongly. God appears in a terrible storm and answers Job out of a whirlwind (chapters 38-39). But, instead of directly answering Job's accusations, God challenges Job:

 Who are you to question my wisdom?...
Were you there when I made the world?...
Do you know all the answers?

Yet this is not a reprimand. God is pleased with 'his servant Job', who, though he may have railed against God, has remained faithful. But for Job's so-called 'comforters' God has sharp words: 'I am angry with you... because you did not speak the truth about me, as my servant Job did.' Despite any apparent evidence to the contrary God is present with, and on the side of, those who suffer.

Thus the book of Job appears to be saying that, from a human perspective, some things must remain a mystery: we do not possess the wisdom of God. There is a purpose behind the suffering but it is not for us to know. The book ends with Job convinced afresh of God's power and his goodness, accepting God's response. He is rewarded with a return to good health and wealth.

As an explanation, many have found the Book of Job to be a frustrating response to the problem it sets out to answer. However, many in the midst of suffering have discerned in Job a wisdom not found in theoretical responses.

Frances Young is the mother of a severely handicapped son. Arthur was born brain-damaged, microcephalic (that is with an abnormally small head). In her book *Face to Face* she tells the story of how she has lived with constant reminders of suffering and yet retained faith in God. It is her testimony to twenty-three years of pain, struggle and love. In it she writes:

> **I had always found the Book of Job baffling when it comes to providing any kind of answer to the problem it raises. When God appears at the end, he does not give any satisfactory explanation. He simply tells Job to contemplate how clever he the Creator is, and suggests that Job should pay his respects – exactly what the comforters had suggested long ago... What satisfies and at the same time humbles Job is simply the reality and presence of God. What God says is irrelevant. In God's presence the demand for explanation ceases. God is sufficient in himself to bring a perspective which transcends and transforms. That is more or less my experience. Face to face with God, the problems do not disappear but they do appear different.**

Some people have attempted to explain suffering by comparing the mystery of it to a tapestry. Look at a tapestry from the wrong side and it seems to be an absolute mess, as though it is completely chaotic. This is how the world often looks, punctured by thousands of examples of suffering. However, when you look at the tapestry from the other side you see order and purpose. So, some people argue that life is like this. The chaos of suffering does have a purpose and meaning.

THINKING IT THROUGH

➡ Job does not give up belief in God but maintains that suffering is beyond his comprehension. Why do you think that some people have found the Book of Job a frustrating and unsatisfactory response to the problem of why good people suffer?

➡ This chapter has raised the whole question of 'innocent suffering'. Do you think there is such a thing?

➡ 'Those who feel God's presence with them in their suffering need no further explanation.' What do you think?

A CASE STUDY: THE HOLOCAUST

Probably more than any other people, the Jews have repeatedly had to face the question of undeserved suffering. Protest to God is enshrined in their scriptures, as the quotation on the right shows.

In a modern translation of the Psalms Jim Cotter continues this psalm, drawing out the connections with the Holocaust:

> The tanks of the mighty encircle me,
> barbed wire and machine guns surround me.
> They have marked my arm with a number,
> and never call me by name.
> They have stripped me of clothes and of shoes,
> and showered me with gas in the chamber of death.
> Why? Why? Why?
> Why, silent God, why?

> My God, my God, why hast thou forsaken me? Why art thou so far from helping me...
> O my God, I cry by day, but thou dost not answer; and by night, but find no rest.

Psalm 22:1-2

The questions raised by the genocidal destruction of Jews in the Second World War loom large in the Jewish community. The numerous memorials to the death camps throughout the world, and especially in Israel, bear witness to a 'Holocaust consciousness or psyche'. During the last fifty years numerous attempts have been made to glimpse some light of understanding in the darkness of this evil destruction.

There are two main approaches to the question of undeserved suffering in face of the Holocaust:

➡ The first is to offer a response – often, but not always, a protest.

➡ The second is to attempt an explanation of the suffering, suggesting a purpose behind it.

RESPONSES TO THE HOLOCAUST

Some responses to the Holocaust have been based on themes found in the Jewish Scriptures.

1. Protesting to God

Protest was Job's response. The sufferer questions God and expresses before God his/her own anxieties, experience of injustice and suffering, feelings of outrage and despair or anger. Many psalms are classic examples of prayers of protest, articulating the human experience and challenging God to do something about it (see margin).

These psalms refuse easy answers. What they do is help us acknowledge the real questions. It is precisely because they confront the questions all of us ask from time to time, that the psalms have such universal appeal.

Because the prayer of protest encourages us to face up to suffering, to come to terms with it by articulating our feelings, it is a useful and cathartic response to the issue of suffering.

Holocaust victim Elie Wiesel responds in a prayer of protest. According to Wiesel we pray to God because he has so much to answer for: we have to protest *against* him as well as *to* him. The only alternative is despair, or silence.

In *A Jew Today* Wiesel describes the one remaining member of a Jewish family saying to God:

 Master of the Universe, I know what you want – I understand what You are doing. You want despair to overwhelm me. You want me to cease believing in You, to cease praying to You, to cease invoking Your name to glorify and sanctify it. Well I tell you: No, no – a thousand times no! You shall not succeed! In spite of me and in spite of You, I shall shout the Kaddish, which is a song of faith, for You and against You. This song You shall not still, God of Israel.

2. Wrestling with God

The second response is to wrestle with God in order to find meaning in the suffering or to justify the innocent. The archetypal story in the Bible is that of Abraham wrestling with God over the fate of Sodom and Gomorrah. The full story is found in Genesis 18. We have reproduced a short extract.

When the men turned and went towards Sodom, Abraham remained standing before the Lord. Abraham drew near him and said, 'Wilt thou really sweep away good and bad together? Suppose there are fifty good men in the city; wilt thou really sweep it away, and not pardon the place because of the fifty good men? Far be it from thee to do this – to kill good and bad together; for then the good would suffer with the bad. Far be it from thee. Shall not the judge of all the earth do what is just?' The Lord said, 'If I find in the city of Sodom fifty good men, I will pardon the whole place for their sake.' Abraham replied, 'May I presume to speak to the Lord, dust and ashes that I am: suppose there are five short of the fifty good men? Wilt thou destroy the whole city for a mere five men?' He said, 'If I find forty-five there I will not destroy it.' Abraham spoke again, 'Suppose forty can be found there?' and he said, 'For the sake of the forty I will not do it.' Then Abraham said, 'Please do not be angry, O Lord, if I speak again: suppose thirty can be found there?' He answered, 'If I find thirty there I will not do it.' Abraham continued, 'May I presume to speak to the Lord: suppose twenty can be found there?' He replied, 'For the sake of the twenty I will not destroy it.' Abraham said, 'I pray thee not to be angry, O Lord, if I speak just once more: suppose ten can be found there?' He said, 'For the sake of the ten I will not destroy it.' When the Lord had finished talking with Abraham, he left him, and Abraham returned home.

These two responses arise out of Jewish Scriptures. Other more practical responses have been:

➡ **To remember** – to bear witness and keep the memory of the dead and the atrocities alive. This memorial is enshrined in such museums as Yad Vashem: it acts as a warning – a witness to the horrors which human beings can inflict on one another.

➡ **To seek justice** – this is exemplified by Simon Wiesenthal, the Nazi hunter. The blood of those slaughtered demands justice: the perpetrators of evil must be brought to trial.

➡ **To bear witness** – people like Primo Levi the novelist aim to bear witness in their writings, and by so doing to learn lessons from the past.

EXPLANATIONS OF THE HOLOCAUST

The second approach to the Holocaust is to attempt to justify the goodness of God in the light of so much suffering. These attempts have been very varied.

One of them has been to talk of a 'God in hiding'. The idea that at times God 'hides his face' when his people suffer is expressed in the Jewish Scriptures:

**'Why do you hide your face,
and forget we are wretched and exploited?'**

Psalm 44:24

E. Berkovits, one of the leading Jewish theologians who offers this idea, writes that God was indeed present in the Holocaust with his chosen people but he was in hiding.

Other Jewish thinkers have suggested that God caused the Holocaust. Maza puts forward the idea that God used the Holocaust as an instrument to return his people to the study of the Torah. This again has echoes in the Bible, where we read of God punishing his people in order to bring them back to himself.

It is wholly understandable that some Jews have lost their faith in God through the orgy of hate they suffered in the Holocaust. However, some have continued to believe, despite all these atrocities – as these words scratched on a cellar wall in Cologne testify:

I believe in the sun even when it is not shining.
I believe in love even when not feeling it.
I believe in God even when he is silent.

➡ How true do you think Wiesel's words are: that we pray to God because he has so much to answer for; that we have to protest against him as well as to him; that the only alternative is despair, or silence?

➡ How does this response differ from that of the person who gives up belief in God because of all the undeserved suffering in the world? Which response do you think is the most credible?

A PURPOSE IN SUFFERING?

*I*n this section we look at a number of quotations which suggest that there may be a purpose in suffering. As you read, try to discover the meaning 'given to' suffering. Have in the back of your mind the question: 'Would the world be a better or worse place without suffering?'

CHARACTER FORMATION THROUGH SUFFERING

Some people suggest that suffering is important in producing depth of character. This is expressed in a number of ways.

Abdul Baha of the Bahai religion puts forward the following idea:

> Suffering can often produce great depths of character, mature understanding, warm compassion and rich spirituality. Of course we should always strive to heal the sick and relieve the oppressed; and we should rejoice that in heaven we shall finally be set free from all pains and tears. But suffering can make us more like Christ. The sparkling radiance of a diamond is caused by a lump of coal subjected to extreme pressure and heat over a long period of time. Again, a beautiful pearl emerges when an oyster has to cover an irritating object with layer upon layer of smooth mother-of-pearl lining excreted from its own body.

David Watson, *Fear No Evil*

At 17 Joni Eareckson broke her neck in a diving accident and was totally paralysed from the neck down.

> The suffering and pain of the past few years had been the ingredients that had helped me mature emotionally, mentally and spiritually. I felt confident and independent, trusting in the Lord for my physical and emotional needs.

Pain and suffering have purpose. We don't always see this clearly. The apostle Paul suffered for Christ. His experience included imprisonment, beatings, stonings, shipwreck and some physical 'thorn in the flesh'. The blessing of suffering is, as J. B. Phillips interprets Romans 5:3-5, '...we can be full of joy here and now even in our trials and troubles. Taken in the right spirit, these very things will give us patient endurance; this in turn will develop a mature

Those who suffer most, attain to the greatest perfection... People who do not suffer, attain no perfection. The plant most pruned by the gardeners is the one which, when the summer comes, will have the most beautiful blossoms and the most abundant fruit.

Quoted in Jan Thompson, *Reflections*

character, and a character of this sort produces a steady hope, a hope that will never disappoint us.'

I believed He was working in my life to create grace and wisdom out of the chaos of pain and depression.

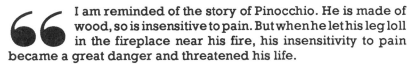

Joni Eareckson, *Joni*

SUFFERING AS A WARNING

Brother Carlo Carretto reflects upon the life of a drug addict he had recently helped while working in Hong Kong:

> I am reminded of the story of Pinocchio. He is made of wood, so is insensitive to pain. But when he let his leg loll in the fireplace near his fire, his insensitivity to pain became a great danger and threatened his life.
>
> It seems absurd to say it, but: what would happen if there were no pain to sensitize us in time, to warn us? What would have stopped the junkie of last night? What would warn the alcoholic of the disorder in which he lives?

Quoted in Jan Thompson, *Reflections*

SUFFERING AS A POTENTIAL RESOURCE

Frances Parsons was a young mother in her twenties when she developed rheumatoid arthritis. Severely crippled, always in great pain, she was at times hardly able to move. In her autobiography, *Pools of Fresh Water*, she writes:

> On the face of it, it would appear that to have spent almost half my life being ill one way or another has been a wretched waste of time, but when I consider that I have experienced illness on organic, structural, depressive and psychic levels, in fact everything but terminal, then I see the accumulated experience as a great wealth to be shared with those who need it.
>
> Some time after Stephen and I began our ministry to the sick, I was listening one day to a tape on which a cathedral choir was singing a collection of psalms, among them Psalm 84. As I listened to the words I was struck by the verse: 'Who going through the vale of misery, use it for a well, and the pools are filled with water.' Suddenly I knew exactly what that meant, at least in the context of my own experience. All those years of pain and suffering had not been wasted but rather were collected in a well to be drawn from whenever there was a thirst... I do not believe in a God who hands out suffering... I do believe, however, that God can and does use suffering... if years of illness and pain had not taught me something of compassionate concern for the sick, then I could never acquire it from professional counselling training.

FRUITS OF SUFFERING

This prayer was found scribbled on a piece of wrapping-paper near the body of a dead child at Ravensbruck concentration camp, one of the Nazi death camps in the Second World War.

O, Lord,
remember not only the men and women of good will,
but also those of evil will.
But do not remember all the suffering
they have inflicted upon us;
remember the fruits we have borne
thanks to this suffering –
our comradeship, our loyalty, our humility,
our courage, our generosity,
the greatness of heart
which has grown out of all this;
and when they come to the judgement,
let all the fruits that we have borne
be their forgiveness.

TURNING TO GOD THROUGH SUFFERING

Some people discover a renewed trust in God when they are undergoing intense suffering.

> It is sometimes only through suffering that we begin to listen to God. Our natural pride and self-confidence have been stripped painfully away, and we become aware, perhaps for the first time, of our own personal needs. We may even begin to ask God for help instead of protesting about our condition or insisting on explanations.
>
> I still do not know why God allowed (my cancer), nor does it bother me. But I am beginning to hear what God is saying, and this has been enormously helpful to me.
>
> I am content to trust myself to a loving God whose control is ultimate and whose wisdom transcends my own feeble understanding.

David Watson, *Fear No Evil*

> Before my accident, I didn't 'need' Christ. Now I needed Him desperately. When I had been on my feet, it never seemed important that He be part of my decision-making – what party to go to, whether to go to a friend's house or

a football game, etc. It didn't seem that He would even be interested in such insignificant things. But, now that my life was reduced to the basic life-routines, He was a part of it because He cared for me. He was, in fact, my only dependable reality.

Joni Eareckson, *Joni*

GIVING SUFFERING A MEANING

> The question we should be asking is not, 'Why did this happen to me? What did I do to deserve this?' That is really an unanswerable, pointless question. A better question would be 'Now that this has happened to me, what am I going to do about it?'
>
> H. Kushner, *When bad things happen to good people*

Suffering so often appears to lack any obvious meaning: it strips people of dignity, leaving many powerless and vulnerable. Many feel that suffering does not have a meaning in itself, but we can give it a meaning. We can redeem the suffering from senselessness.

Dorothee Soelle, in her book *Suffering*, says that 'the most important question we can ask about suffering is whom it serves. Does our suffering serve God or the devil, the cause of becoming alive or being morally paralysed?'

THINKING IT THROUGH

In this chapter we have looked at people who have attempted to make suffering yield meaning – to impose a meaning on it. These are not solutions to the problem of suffering. They are ways of using suffering.

Instead of pointing to meaninglessness in the universe, the existence of suffering could indicate just the opposite, as Richard Holloway believes:

> I have come to believe that the only really compelling argument for the existence of God is the argument *from* suffering. I say argument, but it is no argument; it is deeper than that, it is protest, it is opposition, it is defiance. 'O God, if you do not exist, what becomes of all that suffering? It is wasted, wasted', and I will not believe that, choose not to believe it. If the universe is indifferent to the pains of its children, I rise against the universe and impose my faith upon it. I choose meaning.
> *The Sidelong Glance*

What do you think?

THE SUFFERING GOD

Christianity has 'come at' the problem of suffering from a particular angle. If Jewish theology protests and wrestles with God, Christianity believes in a God who suffers with and for his people. In this section we shall consider what this means.

The following quotation comes from a talk which John Austin Baker gave to dying people at St Christopher's Hospice – people who face day by day the loneliness of death, who cry out in anger 'Why is this happening to me?', 'Why does God make me suffer?'

> There is only one way in which, with the world as it is, God can show himself good in respect of (human) suffering; and that is by not asking of us anything that he is not prepared to endure himself. He must share the dirt and the sweat, the bafflement and the loneliness, the pain, the weakness, yes, and the death too. That would be a God one could respect, a God who put aside all his magic weapons, and did it all as one of us. A God who, when we cry out in our misery (as we all do), 'Why should this happen to me?' can answer truthfully, 'It happened to me too, not because I couldn't help it happening, but because I chose that it should, because it was right.' Then and then alone will our doubts be stilled, not because we understand, but because we can trust.

In her book about Peter Abelard, an important figure in the thirteenth-century church, Helen Waddell recalls a conversation between Peter and his friend Thibault. They are walking in the woods when cries of agony lead them to a rabbit caught in a trap. They free it, but, comforted in Abelard's arms, it dies. Abelard is outraged by its innocent suffering:

> It was that confiding trust that broke Abelard's heart...
>
> 'Thibault,' he said, 'do you think there is a God at all? Whatever has come to me, I earned it. But what did this one do?' Thibault nodded. 'I know,' he said. 'Only I think God is in it too.' Abelard looked up sharply. 'In it? Do you mean that it makes Him suffer the way it does us?' Again Thibault nodded... 'All this,' he stroked the limp body, 'is because of us. But all the time God suffers. More than we do.' Abelard·looked at him, perplexed. 'Thibault, do you mean Calvary?' Thibault shook his

head. 'That was only a piece of it – the piece that we saw – in time. Like that.' He pointed to a fallen tree beside them, sawn through the middle. 'That dark ring there, it goes up and down the whole length of the tree. But you only see it where it is cut across. That is what Christ's life was; the bit of God that we saw. And we think God is like that, because Christ was like that, kind and forgiving sins, and healing people. We think God is like that forever, because it happened once, with Christ. But not the pain. Not the agony at the last. We think that has stopped.' Abelard looked at him... 'Then Thibault,' he said slowly, 'you think that all this...all the pain of the world, was Christ's cross?' 'God's cross,' said Thibault. 'And it goes on.'

In *Face to Face*, in the chapter 'Is God There?', Frances Young writes the following:

There could not be any philosophical answer to the problem of evil; not one is fully satisfactory. The only answer, the only thing that makes it possible to believe in God at all, is the cross... a properly Christian response to the problem of evil has to begin with the cross, with an understanding of atonement. We do not begin by explaining evil away, justifying God, excusing him for the mess he has made of his creation. We begin by contemplating the story which tells of God taking responsibility for the evil in his world, by entering it himself, taking it upon himself, in all its horror, cruelty and pain... At the heart of it all is the cry reported by Mark's Gospel, 'My God, my God, why hast thou forsaken me?' Jesus had experienced even more acutely the abandonment and desolation that I knew in my heart of hearts. It was only because he had that the other side of the story was significant: there in that utter absence of God, was the presence of God.

THE CRUCIFIED CHRIST

The Gospel writers spend a large portion of their time writing about the last week of Jesus' life. This naturally raises the question as to why they thought his death was so important.

The story is one of suffering, but there is an added dimension to this man's suffering. Christians believe that Jesus' death accomplishes a great deal – that it mends the broken relationship between God and humankind brought about by the Fall (see unit 3).

How this can be is essentially a mystery. But the images offered by A.M. Hunter and George Carey provide a glimpse of what Christ has achieved through his death.

Christians believe that Christ, by his self-sacrifice, has brought the ends together, has repaired the broken relationship between humankind and God.

A picture at Catterick Camp, painted during the First World War, shows a signaller lying dead in No-man's-land. He had been sent out to repair a cable broken by shell-fire. There he lies, cold in death, but with his task accomplished; for in his stiffening hands he holds the cable's broken ends together. Beneath the picture stands one pregnant word – 'THROUGH'.

A.M. Hunter, *Introducing the New Testament*

66 In his book *Miracle on the River Kwai*, Ernest Gordon tells of a terrible incident in a World War II Japanese prison camp. The British prisoners were taken back to camp at the end of a hard day's work on the Burma railway. As was customary, the shovels and tools were counted. The Commanding Officer was told that one shovel was missing. The prisoners were lined up and told to produce the missing shovel. No one moved.

The Commanding Officer ordered that a machine gun be trained on the prisoners. 'If the guilty man does not step forward, you will all be shot,' he screamed. Still no one moved. Then, as it looked as if the Commanding Officer was about to give the order to fire, one man stepped forward. He was hustled away and shot. The following day, as the tools were issued, it was found that no shovel was in fact missing; a Japanese soldier had not counted properly.

In a true sense that prisoner died for his friends. Although not guilty, he died as a true substitute. If he had not died perhaps all of them would have. Now clearly this can only be a faint picture of what Jesus did for us. God is no prison camp commander and we are far from innocent. Yet it raises for us an important question: how do we understand the idea of Jesus dying for us? 99

George Carey, *The Lion Handbook of Christian Belief*

'There cannot be a God of love,' men say, 'because if there was, and he looked upon the world, his heart would break.' The Church points to the Cross and says, 'It did break.' 'It is God who made the world,' men say. 'It is he who should bear the load.' The Church points to the Cross and says, 'He did bear it.'

William Temple, quoted in David Watson, *Fear No Evil*

The New Testament speaks of Jesus dying as our substitute, but also as our representative, and as paying the price of our sin (death) to 'buy' our freedom. By dying he made forgiveness possible – making us at-one with God, he suffered as an example to us, and he won a final victory over sin and death. George Carey puts it this way:

66 God personally takes responsibility on himself for the sin, pain, brokenness and suffering of the world, to make it new. He enters into the depth of human suffering. 99

The cross does not answer the question 'Why do people suffer?' Rather, it gives an assurance of one who stands beside us in suffering's depths. Which is more important to the one who suffers?

THE KINGDOM OF GOD

Jesus' life and death reiterate the theme of the creation stories: that God did not intend suffering and conflict to exist. The New Testament teaches that on the cross Jesus paid the price for mankind's rebellion and reversed the effects of the Fall.

Jesus commanded his disciples to go out and proclaim the Kingdom of God, as he had done, in a ministry of healing. Christians continue to do this today. The healing ministry is for the restoration of the person to wholeness, not just physical wholeness, but emotional, spiritual and psychological.

However, Christians believe that the world is still a fallen world in many respects. The Kingdom of God is in its fullest sense yet to come.

> The Bible indicates that our bodies are temporal. Therefore, my paralysis was temporal. When my focus shifted to this eternal perspective, all my concerns about being in a wheelchair became trivial. Although 'condemned' to a wheelchair, I knew one day I'd be free of it.
>
> I believe it's God's will for everyone to be healed. But maybe we just can't agree as to timetable. I believe it is His will, but apparently it doesn't have priority over other things. You will be healed, but probably not until you receive your glorified body.
>
> But God says all of this together can't compare with the glory and future reality He has prepared for me. It's as I said before – the future is the only reality that counts. The only thing we can take to heaven with us is our character. Our character is all we have to determine what kind of a being we will be for all eternity. It's what we *are* that will be tested by fire. Only the qualities of Christ in our character will remain.

Joni Eareckson, *Joni*

GOD WITH US

One of Jesus' names, Immanuel, means 'God with us'. It has been the Christian experience that God is present – in some mysterious way – in the midst of suffering. The God who suffered on the cross continues to suffer in the sufferings of others. This is no theory but a living witness to God's presence. In this section we shall consider what this means through looking at a variety of personal testimonies.

Jesus, my suffering Lord, Grant that today and every day I may see You in the person of Your sick ones, And that in caring for them I may serve You.

Prayer of Mother Teresa, *The Love of Christ*

GOD'S PRESENCE IN SUFFERING

“ There was one particular time when I was very aware of God's stepping in in a very personal way – that was when I'd had yet another operation. I suddenly became aware of God's presence right next to me, in such a close way that I felt as if I could reach out my hand and touch him. After that acute awareness of him being so close… I knew that he still had me very firmly in his hands and that whatever he was to do – whether he decided to allow me to stay as I am, for the time being, or whether he healed me – he was the one who was in control: and I knew that he was to be trusted…

I am really encouraged when people say to me that they have almost glimpsed God in me. It's not because I'm wonderful. It's because God is, and he really is there, and I think that maybe he's asked me to show that he can be with us even when we're going through it. ”

Jane Grayshon, on *Encounter*, ITV, 12.1.91

In her book *HIV Positive* Debra Jarvis has collected together a number of interviews with AIDS patients. One of these spoke in the following way:

“ I had asked God into my life long before I was diagnosed with AIDS. After my diagnosis, some of my friends wondered how I could still believe in God. But God's peace and love are even more evident to me now. I am not saying that I never get scared or lonely. I guess most important is that I know Jesus is right there with me and suffering with me. Sometimes my heart cries out in a language that only God can hear. So my friends are not able to hear those things. But I know that God hears me. ”

Some people have witnessed God's presence in and through other people. David Watson takes Richard Wurmbrand as an example:

> **66** God never promises to save us from adversity, only to be with us in the midst of it. Richard Wurmbrand is a Rumanian pastor who endured fourteen years in various Communist prisons, where he was repeatedly tortured for his faith in Christ. 'They broke four vertebrae in my back and many other bones. They carved me in a dozen places. They burned me and cut eighteen holes in my body.' For three years he was in solitary confinement thirty feet below ground level, during which time the only persons he saw were his torturers. In despair he asked God to speak to him, to say something to him. At that moment he heard a terrible piercing cry. It was from another unfortunate victim who was being tortured. But Wurmbrand heard it as a cry from God's heart. God was revealing what he felt like when he saw his children in pain. 'In all their affliction he was afflicted' (Isaiah 63:9). God shares in our suffering. In that filthy underground prison Wurmbrand discovered a beauty in Christ that he had not known before. He literally danced for joy. **99**

David Watson, *Fear No Evil*

> **66** Pressures seemed greatest at night. Perhaps therapy had gone badly that day. Or no one came to visit. Or maybe Mrs Barber was being mean to me again. Whatever the problem, I'd want to cry. I felt even more frustrated because I couldn't cry, for there was no one to wipe my eyes and help me blow my nose. The Scriptures were encouraging, and I'd apply the reality and truth of them to my own special needs. During these difficult midnight hours, I'd visualize Jesus standing beside my Stryker. I imagined Him as a strong, comforting person with a deep, reassuring voice, saying specifically to me, 'Lo, I am with you always. If I loved you enough to die for you, don't you think I ought to know best how to run your life even if it means your being paralyzed?' The reality of this Scripture was that He was with me, now. Beside me in my own room! That was the comfort I needed.
>
> Jesus did know what it was like not to be able to move – not to be able to scratch your nose, shift your weight, wipe your eyes. *He was paralyzed on the cross.* He could not move His arms or legs. Christ knew exactly how I felt! **99**

Joni Eareckson, *Joni*

> **66** On those terrible children's wards I could neither have worshipped nor respected any God who had not Himself cried, 'My God, my God, why hast Thou forsaken Me?' Only because it was so, only because the Creator loved His creation enough to become helpless with it and suffer in it, totally overwhelmed by the pain of it, I found there was still hope.

Because He Himself has suffered, says the author of the letter to the Hebrews, He is able to help those who suffer now; but not, in my experience, by removing the suffering. The beauty of the twisted tree is still brought out *through* its contortion.

Margaret Spufford, *Celebration*

It has been the experience of many Christians that God suffers alongside his people, and in their suffering gives his peace and love. But, as Margaret Spufford suggests, God is also working in the suffering to transform it and to re-create and redeem it. Frances Young summarizes her faith in the following way:

The cross of Jesus is not just the story of a man being a martyr, but the story of God taking responsibility for all the evil and sin and suffering with which his creation is afflicted, by entering into it and going through it, so that by his presence, the situation may be transformed and recreation begin to happen.

Face to Face

'God himself will be with them; he will wipe away every tear from their eyes, and death shall be no more, neither shall there be mourning nor crying nor pain any more, for the former things have passed away.'

Revelation 21:3-4 expresses the promise of a new creation. This is the Christian's future hope.

FOOTPRINTS

One night a man had a dream. He dreamed he was walking along the beach with the Lord. Across the sky flashed scenes from his life. For each scene he noticed two sets of footprints in the sand: one belonging to him, and the other to the Lord.

When the last scene of his life flashed before him, he looked back at the footprints in the sand. He noticed that many times along the path of his life there was only one set of footprints. He also noticed that it happened at the very lowest and saddest times in his life.

This really bothered him and he questioned the Lord about it. 'Lord, you said that once I decided to follow you, you'd walk with me all the way. But I have noticed that during the most troublesome times in my life, there is only one set of footprints. I don't understand why when I needed you most you would leave me.'

The Lord replied, 'My precious, precious child, I love you and I would never leave you. During your times of trial and suffering, when you see only one set of footprints, it was then that I carried you.'

It is the Christian belief that whilst this transformation can begin here and now it will find its completion when the Kingdom of God is established in its fullness.

THINKING IT THROUGH

Whilst many have felt God's presence with them in their suffering, there are many others who have merely felt alone. If God is in all suffering, why do you think some never experience his presence?

P.S.

I look forward to death with colossal joy.

Malcolm Muggeridge

BEYOND PAIN: THE FUTURE HOPE

Christians believe that suffering and death are not the end of our lot. They look forward to a continuing relationship with God beyond this mortal life. It is this hope which has kept them strong in faith amid the most appalling sufferings. St Paul wrote, 'I consider that the sufferings of this present time are not worth comparing with the glory that is to be revealed to us' (Romans 8:18). He wrote about being 'afflicted… perplexed… persecuted… struck down', yet he could say that 'this slight momentary affliction is preparing for us an eternal weight of glory beyond all comparison' (2 Corinthians 4:17). The secret for Paul was to keep his eyes on the eternal perspective, and this put all personal sufferings into proportion:

 We look not to the things that are seen but to the things that are unseen; for the things that are seen are transient, but the things that are unseen are eternal.

As David Watson writes:

Without this dimension of eternity and without a strong hope in heaven, the problems of our human existence might fill us all with despair. But once we know the love of God for ourselves and believe in life after death – or life *through* death – our outlook on this life, with all its pains and sorrows, can be transformed.

Fear No Evil